I'M more IMPORTANT than my BUSINESS

Whatever happens in the next twelve months,
I will look after myself, and tune in to when I need to take breaks.

I will be kind to myself.
I will pace myself.
I am more important that my business.

A note on planning

What we sow we grow.
Sometimes we plan and it all happens as we laid it out.
But more often than not, what we laid out changes.
Our plan collides with the world within us, and the world around us.
It shapes and bends. We adjust it.
Should we let go of the plan?
NO.
But we let it move, adjust, and we always, always stay focused on the end goal.
The plan is just a plan.
It's the GOALS we keep our eyes on.

(This planner is designed to be a companion to the book
Be a Spider, Build a Web: Sticky Content Marketing for Small Businesses
A "KIND SPIDER" business owner is one who creates a sticky content web, that attracts their ideal clients, creates content that helps them stick around, and trusts the process, allowing those people to come to the 'decision hub' to be sold to, when they are ready.

For more information on how this works, go to beaspiderbuildaweb.com)

We start with us

If we build towards the life we love,

if we build a business that reflects our loves,

our passions, our interests,

if we stay clear on where

we are going,

it all stays simple.

It all builds towards looking

after what is important.

Re-centre your Goals

It's far easier to market a business and offers that we believe in.

Often our reluctance to put ourselves forward, take risks stems from our business model or our offers not quite sitting right.

Perhaps we've added in offers "just because we can" or "because we do a good job of it".
We might be selling what we think people want
And we're not looking at what really fires us up.

This is our business.
We get to choose.
The more we choose what excites us, the easier it is to talk about it.
This makes it easier to grow a thriving business.

My CELEBRATION and LOVE & LIFE Plan

Our lives and our businesses need to reflect what energises
us.
We start with choosing what our priorities are.
We BUILD JOY.

What brings me joy	What can I do to have more of this

My favourite ways to use my time	My self care/"MORE LIFE" priorities this year

My BIG GOALS for the next twelve months

The End Goal

☐ Specific ☐ Meaningful ☐ Aspirational ☐ Risky and Transformational

Milestones

This fits into my big life/business goals because:

This is important because

How I'll feel what achieve it

Barriers I need to overcome

One-off actions I need to take

Regular actions I need to take

My reward:

My BIG GOALS for the next twelve months

The End Goal

☐ Specific ☐ Meaningful ☐ Aspirational ☐ Risky and Transformational

Milestones

This fits into my big life/business goals because:

This is important because

How I'll feel what achieve it

One-off actions I need to take

Barriers I need to overcome

Regular actions I need to take

My reward:

My BIG GOALS for the next twelve months

The End Goal

☐ Specific | ☐ Meaningful | ☐ Aspirational | ☐ Risky and Transformational

Milestones

☐ ☐ ☐

This fits into my big life/business goals because:

This is important because

How I'll feel what achieve it

Barriers I need to overcome

One-off actions I need to take

Regular actions I need to take

My reward:

My BIG GOALS for the next twelve months

The End Goal

☐ Specific   ☐ Meaningful   ☐ Aspirational   ☐ Risky and Transformational

Milestones

☐ ☐ ☐

This fits into my big life/business goals because:

This is important because

How I'll feel what achieve it

Barriers I need to overcome

One-off actions I need to take

Regular actions I need to take

My reward:

My BIG GOALS for the next twelve months

The End Goal

☐ Specific ☐ Meaningful ☐ Aspirational ☐ Risky and Transformational

Milestones

This fits into my big life/business goals because:

This is important because

How I'll feel what achieve it

Barriers I need to overcome

One-off actions I need to take

Regular actions I need to take

My reward:

My BIG GOALS for the next twelve months

The End Goal

☐ Specific   ☐ Meaningful   ☐ Aspirational   ☐ Risky and Transformational

Milestones

☐   ☐   ☐

This fits into my big life/business goals because:

This is important because

How I'll feel what achieve it

Barriers I need to overcome

One-off actions I need to take

Regular actions I need to take

My reward:

A NEW HABIT TO TAKE ACTION

We make habits to make our goals possible. To build habits we need to make space for them in our life.

Priority habit	FREQUENCY
Why I need to build this	Impact to my business/goals

How this fits into existing routine	What needs to be in place first

STEPS TO CREATING THIS HABIT

1.   4.

2.   5.

3.   6.

My reward	Dopamine hunting (motivation)

A NEW HABIT TO TAKE ACTION

We make habits to make our goals possible. To build habits we need to make space for them in our life.

Priority habit	FREQUENCY
Why I need to build this	Impact to my business/goals

How this fits into existing routine	What needs to be in place first

STEPS TO CREATING THIS HABIT

1.   4.
2.   5.
3.   6.

My reward	Dopamine hunting (motivation)

A NEW HABIT TO TAKE ACTION

We make habits to make our goals possible. To build habits we need to make space for them in our life.

Priority habit	FREQUENCY
Why I need to build this	Impact to my business/goals

How this fits into existing routine	What needs to be in place first

STEPS TO CREATING THIS HABIT

1.   4.
2.   5.
3.   6.

My reward	Dopamine hunting (motivation)

A NEW HABIT TO TAKE ACTION

We make habits to make our goals possible. To build habits we need to make space for them in our life.

Priority habit	FREQUENCY
Why I need to build this	Impact to my business/goals

How this fits into existing routine	What needs to be in place first

STEPS TO CREATING THIS HABIT

1.   4.

2.   5.

3.   6.

My reward	Dopamine hunting (motivation)

A NEW HABIT TO TAKE ACTION

We make habits to make our goals possible. To build habits we need to make space for them in our life.

Priority habit	FREQUENCY
Why I need to build this	Impact to my business/goals

How this fits into existing routine	What needs to be in place first

STEPS TO CREATING THIS HABIT

1.   4.
2.   5.
3.   6.

My reward	Dopamine hunting (motivation)

A NEW HABIT TO TAKE ACTION

We make habits to make our goals possible. To build habits we need to make space for them in our life.

Priority habit	FREQUENCY
Why I need to build this	Impact to my business/goals

How this fits into existing routine	What needs to be in place first

STEPS TO CREATING THIS HABIT

1.
2.
3.

4.
5.
6.

My reward	Dopamine hunting (motivation)

Sale goals this year

My turn over goal is:

My ideal customers value over a year is:

Offers sales goal

OFFER	PRICE	NUMBERS SOLD	VALUE	% GOAL

My sale goals/QTR

Q1	Q2	Q3	Q4

My marketing health actions

Weekly

- Prioritising SALES ACTIVITY
- Responding to Email/Messages/Comments
- Keeping marketing time for marketing

Monthly

- Block out marketing times
- Batch content for month
- Look over analytics and note changes
- Record leads/sales information
- Do something "Fun"

Quarterly

- Note what worked/didn't work
- Repeat post topics that really worked
- Make space for new habits/new learning
- Check progress against goals
- Reset/create goals

Annually

- Check PRICING
- Check offer
- Check messaging
- Update website
- Brand Photography
- Create new lead generation
- Tidy up Email list
- Create fresh templates

- Update/ rework all social media profiles
- Update email signature

Plan for next year.

QUARTERLY PLAN FOR DEVELOPMENT

Select one learning, one performance, one personal

Q1	Q2	Q3	Q4

30|60|90	MY GOAL	MY ACTIONS	MY RESULT
NEXT 30 DAYS			
30 - 60 DAYS			
60 - 90 DAYS			

My weekly plan

| Q1 | Q2 | Q3 | Q4 |

My time blocks for:

- Selfcare
- Planning
- Marketing

- Connection
- Work
- Client/customers

- Sales
- Team

TIP:
COLOUR COOL FOR ME, MY
LIFE MY NETWORK/FAMILY
MY BUSINESS

🕐	Monday	Tuesday	Wednesday
7			
8			
9			
10			
11			
12			
1			
2			
3			
4			
5			
6			
7			

🕐	Thursday	Friday	Saturday
7			
8			
9			
10			
11			
12			Sunday
1			
2			
3			
4			
5			
6			
7			

QUARTERLY PLAN FOR DEVELOPMENT

Select one learning, one performance, one personal

	Q1	Q2	Q3	Q4

30|60|90	MY GOAL	MY ACTIONS	MY RESULT
NEXT 30 DAYS			
30 - 60 DAYS			
60 - 90 DAYS			

My weekly plan

| Q1 | Q2 | Q3 | Q4 |

My time blocks for:

- Selfcare
- Planning
- Marketing

- Connection
- Work
- Client/customers

- Sales
- Team

TIP:
COLOUR COOL FOR ME, MY
LIFE MY NETWORK/FAMILY
MY BUSINESS

🕐	Monday	Tuesday	Wednesday
7 8 9 10 11 12 1 2 3 4 5 6 7			

🕐	Thursday	Friday	Saturday
7 8 9 10 11 12 1 2 3 4 5 6 7			Sunday

QUARTERLY PLAN FOR DEVELOPMENT

	Q1	Q2	Q3	Q4

Select one learning, one performance, one personal

30|60|90	MY GOAL	MY ACTIONS	MY RESULT
NEXT 30 DAYS			
30 - 60 DAYS			
60 - 90 DAYS			

My weekly plan

| Q1 | Q2 | Q3 | Q4 |

My time blocks for:

- Selfcare
- Planning
- Marketing
- Connection
- Work
- Client/customers
- Sales
- Team

TIP:
COLOUR COOL FOR ME, MY
LIFE MY NETWORK/FAMILY
MY BUSINESS

	Monday	Tuesday	Wednesday
7 8 9 10 11 12 1 2 3 4 5 6 7			

	Thursday	Friday	Saturday
7 8 9 10 11 12 1 2 3 4 5 6 7			Sunday

QUARTERLY PLAN FOR DEVELOPMENT

	Q1	Q2	Q3	Q4

Select one learning, one performance, one personal

30|60|90	MY GOAL	MY ACTIONS	MY RESULT
NEXT 30 DAYS			
30 - 60 DAYS			
60 - 90 DAYS			

My weekly plan

My time blocks for:

- Selfcare
- Planning
- Marketing
- Connection
- Work
- Client/customers
- Sales
- Team

TIP:
COLOUR COOL FOR ME, MY
LIFE MY NETWORK/FAMILY
MY BUSINESS

🕐	Monday	Tuesday	Wednesday
7 8 9 10 11 12 1 2 3 4 5 6 7			

🕐	Thursday	Friday	Saturday
7 8 9 10 11 12 1 2 3 4 5 6 7			Sunday

My Marketing Foundations

Narrow your offer

We don't need to talk about everything we do in our marketing.

*In fact, we **shouldn't** talk about it all.*

We want people to know what we are here for,
so we make it easy for them by only giving them a few things to know.

We want to make our marketing simple,
so we choose our most important offers to focus on.

Choose what fires you up most
Choose what is most profitable.
Choose what leads to more work/purchases.

This can take a while to work out.
But it is worth it!

We want to "NARROW THE ARROW"

My ICEBERG OFFERS

Make selective choices about what you SHOW in your
marketing as your core offers

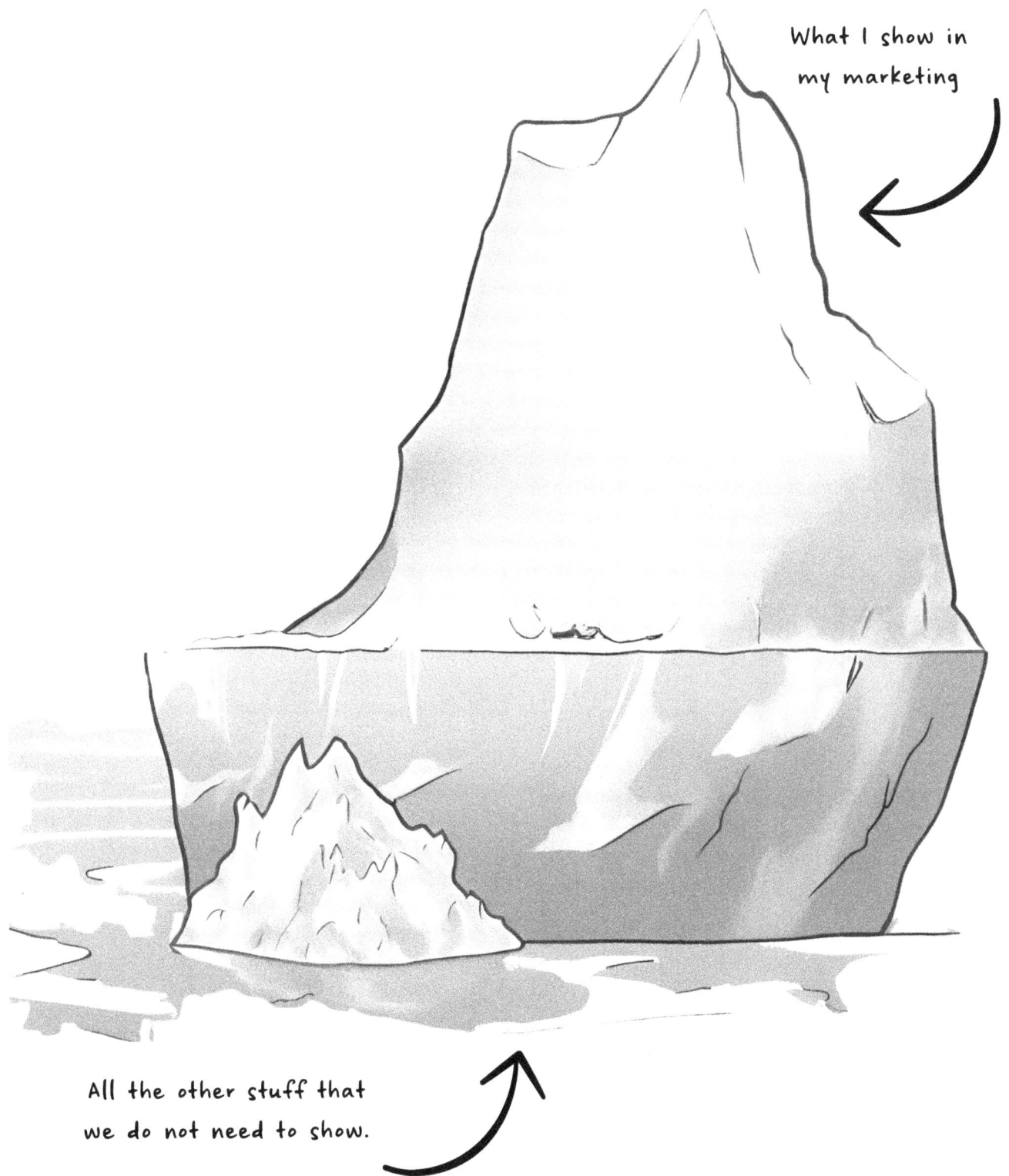

What I show in
my marketing

All the other stuff that
we do not need to show.

Narrow your audience

When we try to talk to everyone, no one notices us .
We end up talking to no one.

The world is noisy, and we've got to get really specific on who we are talking to and why they need us.

For small business owners, focusing on demographics often doesn't help us reach our ideal audience (when it comes to content marketing).

Our job is to work out who is most ready for us, and then talk to them

We talk to the beliefs our audience already hold.
We show them how we can meet their needs.
We show them the outcome they are searching for.

(Limiting your number of audiences makes marketing easier)

My ideal customer

What they believe about themselves	What they need to believe/know about me the business
What NEEDS do we meet for them?	**What OUTCOME are they seeking?**

My ideal customer

What they believe about themselves	What they need to believe/know about me the business
What NEEDS do we meet for them?	What OUTCOME are they seeking?

My ideal customer

What they believe about themselves	What they need to believe/know about me the business
What NEEDS do we meet for them?	**What OUTCOME are they seeking?**

Build your content plan

Our content plan is designed to make it simpler to create content.

It's what you need to focus on in your content creation times.

We use the overall plan to create content for each stage of the content marketing journey.

We use our list of tens to give us an outline of the content we'll talk about, so when it comes to creating our content we stay on track, we don't wase energy trying to think of topics, and we can be assured everything we create will draw our ideal customer closer.

HINT: For your three subsections you can:
Focus on three offers
Focus on three core audiences
Focus on the before, during and after of working with you/ buying from you

My CONTENT MARKETING PROGRESS

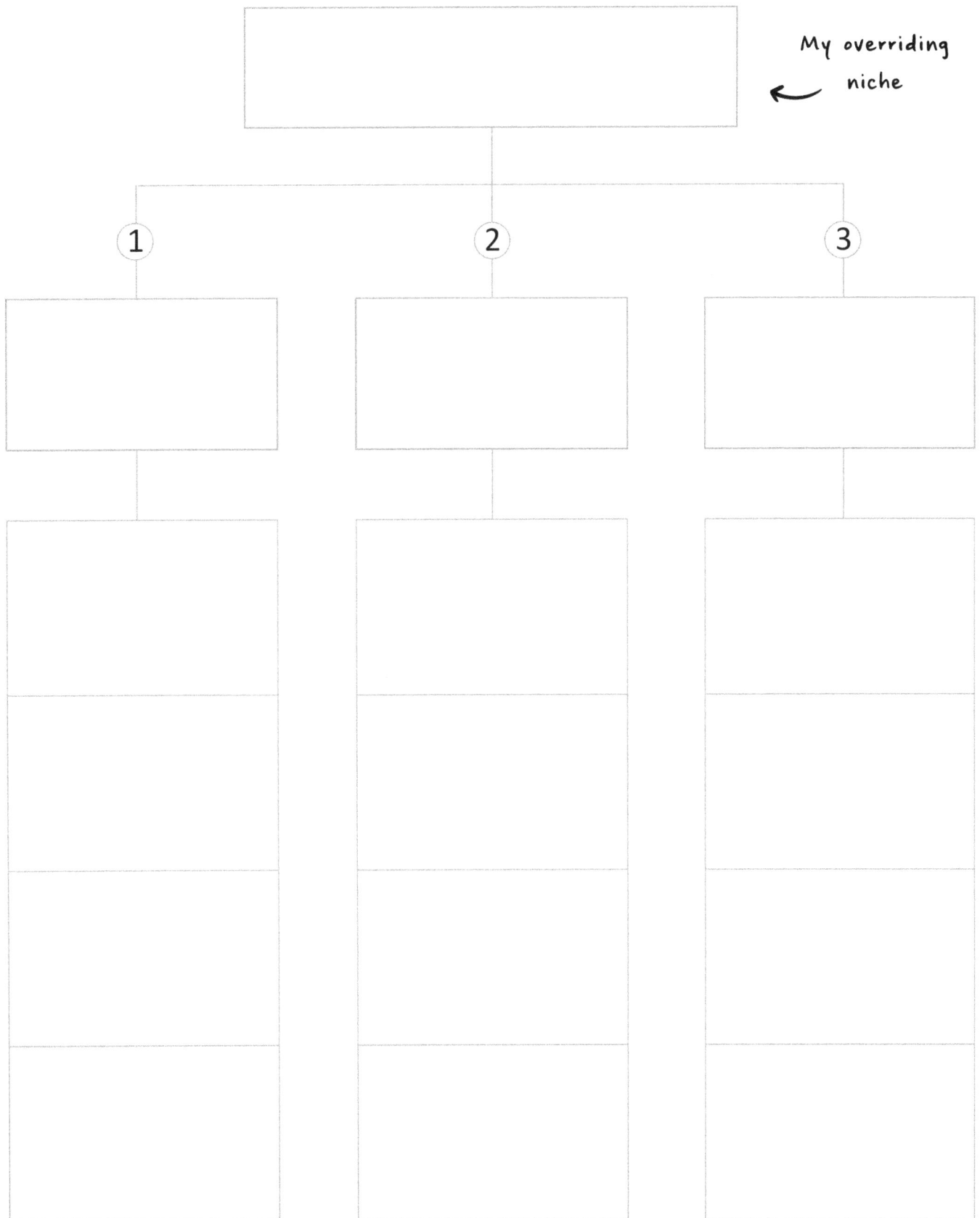

My overriding
niche ←

1

2

3

REMEMBER:
We only talk about what excites us, energises us, and fits what we sell that meets our customers needs.

My lists of tens

CORE OFFER:

FAQ/QUESTIONS	CLIENT STORIES/ TESTIMONIALS
1	1
2	2
3	3
4	4
5	5
6	6
7	7
8	8
9	9
10	10

BENEFITS/WAYS OF WORKING	HIGH INTEREST TOPIC
1	1
2	2
3	3
4	4
5	5
6	6
7	7
8	8
9	9
10	10

My lists of tens

CORE OFFER:

FAQ/QUESTIONS	CLIENT STORIES/ TESTIMONIALS
1	1
2	2
3	3
4	4
5	5
6	6
7	7
8	8
9	9
10	10
BENEFITS/WAYS OF WORKING	HIGH INTEREST TOPIC
1	1
2	2
3	3
4	4
5	5
6	6
7	7
8	8
9	9
10	10

My lists of tens

CORE OFFER:

FAQ/QUESTIONS	CLIENT STORIES/ TESTIMONIALS
1	1
2	2
3	3
4	4
5	5
6	6
7	7
8	8
9	9
10	10
BENEFITS/WAYS OF WORKING	**HIGH INTEREST TOPIC**
1	1
2	2
3	3
4	4
5	5
6	6
7	7
8	8
9	9
10	10

THE
CONTENT
MASTERWEB
FRAMEWORK

We are building a
STICKY WEB.

Acting on your plan

A sticky web attracts, engages and then converts our ideal customers.

We need to use the mix of different activity both online and offline to help make this web interesting and captivating enough to stay sticky.

We want to be "kind spiders" who allow our ideal customers to come, hang out and feel safe with us until they are ready to buy.

We don't need to JUMP on them when they come onto our web.

We trust them to come to us
But we also make that easy by giving them content they'll want to hang around for.

Your Website, Email, and Social Media are your sticky web online
What does yours look like?

My STICKY WEB.

Draw out your sticky web of activity - include your website and email marketing

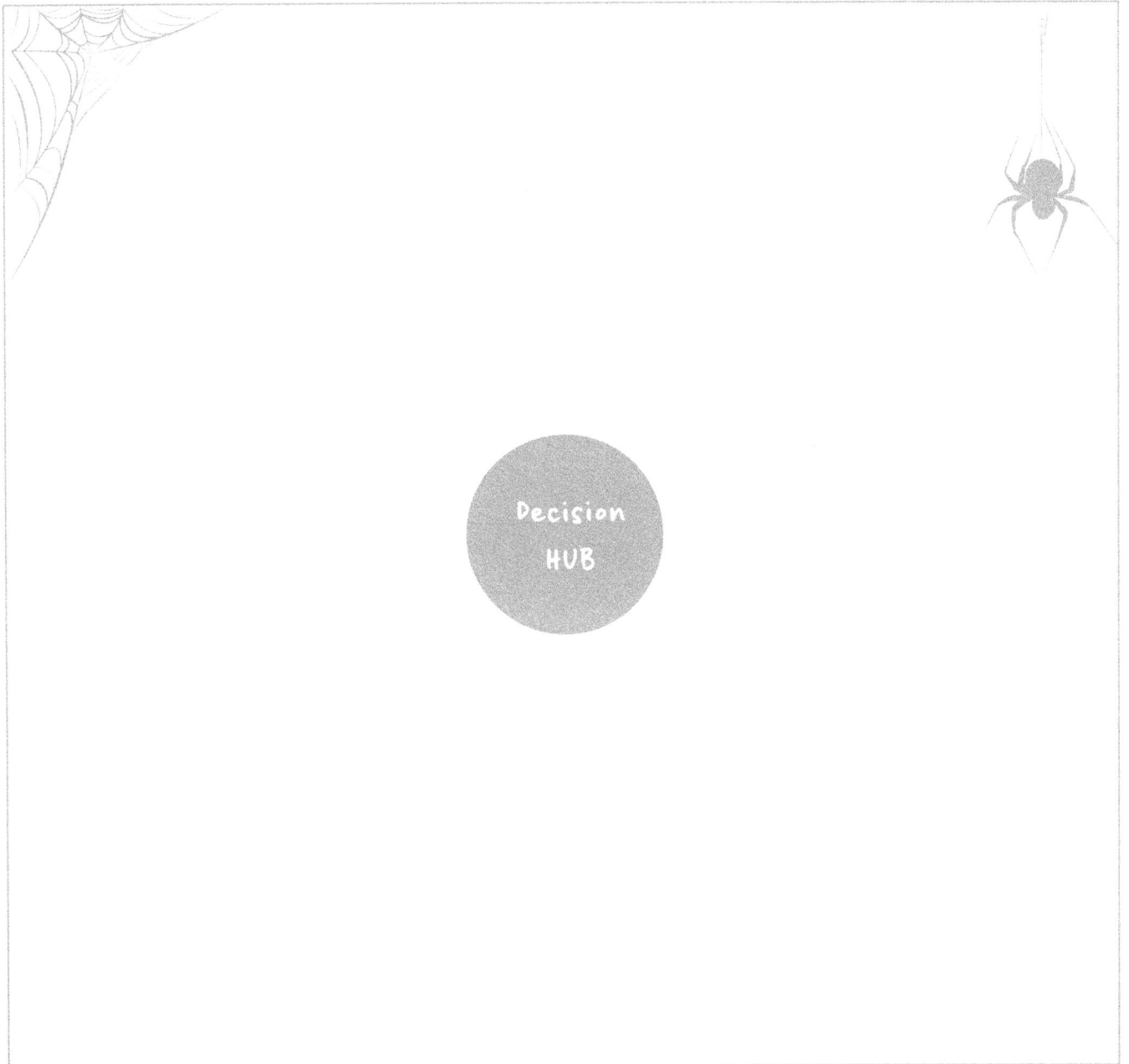

Decision HUB

My CONTENT MARKETING PROGRESS
(WE START AT THE BOTTOM. WE WORK UP!)

End

**NOTICED
(REACH)**

- [ ] Chosen MOTIVATING, EDUCATING, CONTROVERSIAL, ENTERTAINING.
- [ ] Use list of tens in LIGHT Way.
- [ ] Using MEMES /VIDEO/CAROUSEL/TOPICAL Content.
- [ ] Have regular schedule.

**CONNECTED
(AUTHORITY)**

- [ ] Have "expert advice" you love to share.
- [ ] Use list of tens to stay focused.
- [ ] Focused on showing your expertise.
- [ ] Linking to client stories/personal story.
- [ ] Scheduling into your content.

**NURTURED
(CONFIDENCE)**

- [ ] Know your chosen "personable" topics.
- [ ] Have structured times to share.
- [ ] Choosing your style.
- [ ] Creating content.
- [ ] Scheduling it.

**YOURS
(READY TO BUY)**

- [ ] I Have a clear offer/offers.
- [ ] Have planned out 5/6 regular promotional posts.
- [ ] Have designed completed posts.
- [ ] Have scheduled on repeat.

**COMMUNITY
(EMAIL)**

- [ ] Have my email list/have segmented.
- [ ] Have an email plan.
- [ ] Have an email habit.
- [ ] Increased engagement.
- [ ] Getting leads and sales from email.

Start

CONTENT that ENERGISES ME

Content that I love to talk about

Content that people respond to

Content that brings in sales

THE DISCARD LIST.
(Content that makes me bored/disengaged)

My MARKETING HEALTH ACTIONS

HOOKS

CALL TO ACTIONS

MY
QUARTERLY
ACTIVITY

Q1	Q2	Q3	Q4

Content/ Keywords/ Hashtags

Q1	Q2	Q3	Q4

Content themes and ideas I'm focusing on

Keywords I need to use

Hashtag Bank

WEEKLY PLAN

	Q1	Q2	Q3	Q4

Platform	Mon	Tues	Wed	Thurs	Fri	Sat	Sun
Email							

MY EMAIL PLAN

Q1	Q2	Q3	Q4

THE FOUR STEP PLAN

All emails need:
- ○ A short story
- ○ One call to action
- ○ Kept simple
- ○ Add value
- ○ Personalised it

WHAT IS MY SALE FOCUS?

	Offer	%
1.		
2.		
3.		
4.		

My email focus	Tone/style	Offer/CTA
Week 1/5/9		
Week 2/6/10		
Week 3/7/11		
Week 4/8/12		

MY EMAIL PLAN

Q1	Q2	Q3	Q4

THE FOUR STEP PLAN

All emails need:
- ○ A short story
- ○ One call to action
- ○ Kept simple
- ○ Add value
- ○ Personalised it

WHAT IS MY SALE FOCUS?

Offer   %

1.

2.

3.

4.

My email focus	Tone/style	Offer/CTA
Week 1/5/9		
Week 2/6/10		
Week 3/7/11		
Week 4/8/12		

MY EMAIL PLAN

Q1	Q2	Q3	Q4

THE FOUR STEP PLAN

All emails need:
- ○ A short story
- ○ One call to action
- ○ Kept simple
- ○ Add value
- ○ Personalised it

WHAT IS MY SALE FOCUS?

Offer   %

1.

2.

3.

4.

My email focus	Tone/style	Offer/CTA
Week 1/5/9		
Week 2/6/10		
Week 3/7/11		
Week 4/8/12		

My core platform schedule

Platform	
Frequency	

Q1	Q2	Q3	Q4

Day of week	Time	Type	Format
Monday			
Tuesday			
Wednesday			
Thursday			
Friday			
Saturday			
Sunday			

Type:
Promo
FAQ
Social proof
How we work
About us
Relational Content
Reach/Noticed

Formats:
Carousel
Single Image in text
Meme
Video
Quotes
Testimonials
Reels/Short video
Animation

My MONTHLY ACTIVITY TRACKER

J F M A M J J A S O N D

Working ahead keeps us ON TRACK and IN CONTROL. Tick off as you work ahead.

Content type	Frequency	1	2	3	4	5	Date done
		☐	☐	☐	☐	☐	
		☐	☐	☐	☐	☐	
		☐	☐	☐	☐	☐	
		☐	☐	☐	☐	☐	
		☐	☐	☐	☐	☐	
		☐	☐	☐	☐	☐	
		☐	☐	☐	☐	☐	
		☐	☐	☐	☐	☐	
		☐	☐	☐	☐	☐	
		☐	☐	☐	☐	☐	
		☐	☐	☐	☐	☐	
		☐	☐	☐	☐	☐	
		☐	☐	☐	☐	☐	

My MONTHLY PLAN

J F M A M J J A S O N D

GRATITUDE FOCUS FOR MONTH

1.

2.

3.

BRAIN DUMP

FOR THIS MONTH (THIS IS MY SAFE SPACE!)

THIS MONTH PRIORITES

FOR IMPACT THIS MONTH	FOR IMPACT NEXT MONTH
FOR IMPACT THIS QUARTER	FOR IMPACT LONGER TERM

My MONTHLY ACTIVITY TRACKER

J F M A M J J A S O N D

Working ahead keeps us ON TRACK and IN CONTROL. Tick off as you work ahead.

Content type	Frequency	1	2	3	4	5	Date done
		☐	☐	☐	☐	☐	
		☐	☐	☐	☐	☐	
		☐	☐	☐	☐	☐	
		☐	☐	☐	☐	☐	
		☐	☐	☐	☐	☐	
		☐	☐	☐	☐	☐	
		☐	☐	☐	☐	☐	
		☐	☐	☐	☐	☐	
		☐	☐	☐	☐	☐	
		☐	☐	☐	☐	☐	
		☐	☐	☐	☐	☐	
		☐	☐	☐	☐	☐	
		☐	☐	☐	☐	☐	

My MONTHLY PLAN

J F M A M J J A S O N D

GRATITUDE FOCUS FOR MONTH

1. ....

2. ....

3. ....

BRAIN DUMP

FOR THIS MONTH (THIS IS MY SAFE SPACE!)

THIS MONTH PRIORITES

FOR IMPACT THIS MONTH	FOR IMPACT NEXT MONTH
FOR IMPACT THIS QUARTER	FOR IMPACT LONGER TERM

My MONTHLY ACTIVITY TRACKER

J F M A M J J A S O N D

Working ahead keeps us ON TRACK and IN CONTROL. Tick off as you work ahead.

Content type	Frequency	1	2	3	4	5	Date done
		☐	☐	☐	☐	☐	
		☐	☐	☐	☐	☐	
		☐	☐	☐	☐	☐	
		☐	☐	☐	☐	☐	
		☐	☐	☐	☐	☐	
		☐	☐	☐	☐	☐	
		☐	☐	☐	☐	☐	
		☐	☐	☐	☐	☐	
		☐	☐	☐	☐	☐	
		☐	☐	☐	☐	☐	
		☐	☐	☐	☐	☐	
		☐	☐	☐	☐	☐	
		☐	☐	☐	☐	☐	
		☐	☐	☐	☐	☐	

My MONTHLY PLAN

J F M A M J J A S O N D

GRATITUDE FOCUS FOR MONTH

1.
2.
3.

BRAIN DUMP

FOR THIS MONTH (THIS IS MY SAFE SPACE!)

THIS MONTH PRIORITES

FOR IMPACT THIS MONTH	FOR IMPACT NEXT MONTH
FOR IMPACT THIS QUARTER	FOR IMPACT LONGER TERM

MY QUARTERLY REFLECTION

Activity or goals I had to postpone during this quarter

THINGS that I need to try next quarter

MY QUARTERLY ACTIVITY

Q1	Q2	Q3	Q4

Content/ Keywords/ Hashtags

Q1	Q2	Q3	Q4

Content themes and ideas I'm focusing on

Keywords I need to use

Hashtag Bank

WEEKLY PLAN

Platform	Mon	Tues	Wed	Thurs	Fri	Sat	Sun
Email							

Q1	Q2	Q3	Q4

MY EMAIL PLAN

Q1	Q2	Q3	Q4

THE FOUR STEP PLAN

All emails need:
- ○ A short story
- ○ One call to action
- ○ Kept simple
- ○ Add value
- ○ Personalised it

WHAT IS MY SALE FOCUS?

Offer   %

1.

2.

3.

4.

My email focus	Tone/style	Offer/CTA
Week 1/5/9		
Week 2/6/10		
Week 3/7/11		
Week 4/8/12		

MY EMAIL PLAN

Q1	Q2	Q3	Q4

THE FOUR STEP PLAN

All emails need:
- ○ A short story
- ○ One call to action
- ○ Kept simple
- ○ Add value
- ○ Personalised it

WHAT IS MY SALE FOCUS?

Offer   %

1.

2.

3.

4.

My email focus	Tone/style	Offer/CTA
Week 1/5/9		
Week 2/6/10		
Week 3/7/11		
Week 4/8/12		

MY EMAIL PLAN

Q1	Q2	Q3	Q4

THE FOUR STEP PLAN

All emails need:
- ○ A short story
- ○ One call to action
- ○ Kept simple
- ○ Add value
- ○ Personalised it

WHAT IS MY SALE FOCUS?

Offer   %

1.

2.

3.

4.

My email focus	Tone/style	Offer/CTA
Week 1/5/9		
Week 2/6/10		
Week 3/7/11		
Week 4/8/12		

My core platform schedule

Platform	
Frequency	

Q1	Q2	Q3	Q4

Day of week	Time	Type	Format
Monday			
Tuesday			
Wednesday			
Thursday			
Friday			
Saturday			
Sunday			

Type:		Formats:	
	Promo		Carousel
	FAQ		Single Image in text
	Social proof		Meme
	How we work		Video
	About us		Quotes
	Relational Content		Testimonials
	Reach/Noticed		Reels/Short video
			Animation

My MONTHLY ACTIVITY TRACKER

J F M A M J J A S O N D

Working ahead keeps us ON TRACK and IN CONTROL. Tick off as you work ahead.

Content type	Frequency	1	2	3	4	5	Date done
		☐	☐	☐	☐	☐	
		☐	☐	☐	☐	☐	
		☐	☐	☐	☐	☐	
		☐	☐	☐	☐	☐	
		☐	☐	☐	☐	☐	
		☐	☐	☐	☐	☐	
		☐	☐	☐	☐	☐	
		☐	☐	☐	☐	☐	
		☐	☐	☐	☐	☐	
		☐	☐	☐	☐	☐	
		☐	☐	☐	☐	☐	
		☐	☐	☐	☐	☐	
		☐	☐	☐	☐	☐	

My MONTHLY PLAN

J F M A M J J A S O N D

GRATITUDE FOCUS FOR MONTH

1.
2.
3.

BRAIN DUMP

FOR THIS MONTH (THIS IS MY SAFE SPACE!)

THIS MONTH PRIORITES

FOR IMPACT THIS MONTH	FOR IMPACT NEXT MONTH
FOR IMPACT THIS QUARTER	FOR IMPACT LONGER TERM

My MONTHLY ACTIVITY TRACKER

J F M A M J J A S O N D

Working ahead keeps us ON TRACK and IN CONTROL. Tick off as you work ahead.

Content type	Frequency	1	2	3	4	5	Date done
		☐	☐	☐	☐	☐	
		☐	☐	☐	☐	☐	
		☐	☐	☐	☐	☐	
		☐	☐	☐	☐	☐	
		☐	☐	☐	☐	☐	
		☐	☐	☐	☐	☐	
		☐	☐	☐	☐	☐	
		☐	☐	☐	☐	☐	
		☐	☐	☐	☐	☐	
		☐	☐	☐	☐	☐	
		☐	☐	☐	☐	☐	
		☐	☐	☐	☐	☐	
		☐	☐	☐	☐	☐	
		☐	☐	☐	☐	☐	

My MONTHLY PLAN

J F M A M J J A S O N D

GRATITUDE FOCUS FOR MONTH

1.

2.

3.

BRAIN DUMP

FOR THIS MONTH (THIS IS MY SAFE SPACE!)

THIS MONTH PRIORITES

FOR IMPACT THIS MONTH	FOR IMPACT NEXT MONTH
FOR IMPACT THIS QUARTER	FOR IMPACT LONGER TERM

My MONTHLY ACTIVITY TRACKER

J F M A M J J A S O N D

Working ahead keeps us ON TRACK and IN CONTROL. Tick off as you work ahead.

Content type	Frequency	1	2	3	4	5	Date done
		☐	☐	☐	☐	☐	
		☐	☐	☐	☐	☐	
		☐	☐	☐	☐	☐	
		☐	☐	☐	☐	☐	
		☐	☐	☐	☐	☐	
		☐	☐	☐	☐	☐	
		☐	☐	☐	☐	☐	
		☐	☐	☐	☐	☐	
		☐	☐	☐	☐	☐	
		☐	☐	☐	☐	☐	
		☐	☐	☐	☐	☐	
		☐	☐	☐	☐	☐	
		☐	☐	☐	☐	☐	

My MONTHLY PLAN

J F M A M J J A S O N D

GRATITUDE FOCUS FOR MONTH

1.
2.
3.

BRAIN DUMP

FOR THIS MONTH (THIS IS MY SAFE SPACE!)

THIS MONTH PRIORITES

FOR IMPACT THIS MONTH	FOR IMPACT NEXT MONTH
FOR IMPACT THIS QUARTER	FOR IMPACT LONGER TERM

MY QUARTERLY REFLECTION

Activity or goals I had to postpone during this quarter

THINGS that I need to try next quarter

MY
QUARTERLY
ACTIVITY

Q1	Q2	Q3	Q4

Content/ Keywords/ Hashtags

Q1	Q2	Q3	Q4

Content themes and ideas I'm focusing on

Keywords I need to use

Hashtag Bank

WEEKLY PLAN

Platform	Mon	Tues	Wed	Thurs	Fri	Sat	Sun
Email							

Q1	Q2	Q3	Q4

MY EMAIL PLAN

Q1	Q2	Q3	Q4

THE FOUR STEP PLAN

All emails need:
- ○ A short story
- ○ One call to action
- ○ Kept simple
- ○ Add value
- ○ Personalised it

WHAT IS MY SALE FOCUS?

Offer   %

1.

2.

3.

4.

My email focus	Tone/style	Offer/CTA
Week 1/5/9		
Week 2/6/10		
Week 3/7/11		
Week 4/8/12		

MY EMAIL PLAN

Q1	Q2	Q3	Q4

THE FOUR STEP PLAN

All emails need:
- ○ A short story
- ○ One call to action
- ○ Kept simple
- ○ Add value
- ○ Personalised it

WHAT IS MY SALE FOCUS?

Offer   %

1.

2.

3.

4.

My email focus	Tone/style	Offer/CTA
Week 1/5/9		
Week 2/6/10		
Week 3/7/11		
Week 4/8/12		

MY EMAIL PLAN

Q1	Q2	Q3	Q4

THE FOUR STEP PLAN

All emails need:
- ○ A short story
- ○ One call to action
- ○ Kept simple
- ○ Add value
- ○ Personalised it

WHAT IS MY SALE FOCUS?

Offer   %

1.

2.

3.

4.

My email focus	Tone/style	Offer/CTA
Week 1/5/9		
Week 2/6/10		
Week 3/7/11		
Week 4/8/12		

My core platform schedule

Platform	
Frequency	

Q1	Q2	Q3	Q4

Day of week	Time	Type	Format
Monday			
Tuesday			
Wednesday			
Thursday			
Friday			
Saturday			
Sunday			

Type:
Promo
FAQ
Social proof
How we work
About us
Relational Content
Reach/Noticed

Formats:
Carousel
Single Image in text
Meme
Video
Quotes
Testimonials
Reels/Short video
Animation

My MONTHLY ACTIVITY TRACKER

J F M A M J J A S O N D

Working ahead keeps us ON TRACK and IN CONTROL. Tick off as you work ahead.

Content type	Frequency	1	2	3	4	5	Date done
		☐	☐	☐	☐	☐	
		☐	☐	☐	☐	☐	
		☐	☐	☐	☐	☐	
		☐	☐	☐	☐	☐	
		☐	☐	☐	☐	☐	
		☐	☐	☐	☐	☐	
		☐	☐	☐	☐	☐	
		☐	☐	☐	☐	☐	
		☐	☐	☐	☐	☐	
		☐	☐	☐	☐	☐	
		☐	☐	☐	☐	☐	
		☐	☐	☐	☐	☐	
		☐	☐	☐	☐	☐	
		☐	☐	☐	☐	☐	

My MONTHLY PLAN

J F M A M J J A S O N D

GRATITUDE FOCUS FOR MONTH

1.
2.
3.

BRAIN DUMP

FOR THIS MONTH (THIS IS MY SAFE SPACE!)

THIS MONTH PRIORITES

FOR IMPACT THIS MONTH	FOR IMPACT NEXT MONTH
FOR IMPACT THIS QUARTER	FOR IMPACT LONGER TERM

My MONTHLY ACTIVITY TRACKER

J F M A M J J A S O N D

Working ahead keeps us ON TRACK and IN CONTROL. Tick off as you work ahead.

Content type	Frequency	1	2	3	4	5	Date done
		☐	☐	☐	☐	☐	
		☐	☐	☐	☐	☐	
		☐	☐	☐	☐	☐	
		☐	☐	☐	☐	☐	
		☐	☐	☐	☐	☐	
		☐	☐	☐	☐	☐	
		☐	☐	☐	☐	☐	
		☐	☐	☐	☐	☐	
		☐	☐	☐	☐	☐	
		☐	☐	☐	☐	☐	
		☐	☐	☐	☐	☐	
		☐	☐	☐	☐	☐	
		☐	☐	☐	☐	☐	
		☐	☐	☐	☐	☐	

My MONTHLY PLAN

J F M A M J J A S O N D

GRATITUDE FOCUS FOR MONTH

1.
2.
3.

BRAIN DUMP

FOR THIS MONTH (THIS IS MY SAFE SPACE!)

THIS MONTH PRIORITES

FOR IMPACT THIS MONTH	FOR IMPACT NEXT MONTH
FOR IMPACT THIS QUARTER	FOR IMPACT LONGER TERM

My MONTHLY ACTIVITY TRACKER

J F M A M J J A S O N D

Working ahead keeps us ON TRACK and IN CONTROL. Tick off as you work ahead.

Content type	Frequency	1	2	3	4	5	Date done
		☐	☐	☐	☐	☐	
		☐	☐	☐	☐	☐	
		☐	☐	☐	☐	☐	
		☐	☐	☐	☐	☐	
		☐	☐	☐	☐	☐	
		☐	☐	☐	☐	☐	
		☐	☐	☐	☐	☐	
		☐	☐	☐	☐	☐	
		☐	☐	☐	☐	☐	
		☐	☐	☐	☐	☐	
		☐	☐	☐	☐	☐	
		☐	☐	☐	☐	☐	
		☐	☐	☐	☐	☐	
		☐	☐	☐	☐	☐	

My MONTHLY PLAN

J F M A M J J A S O N D

GRATITUDE FOCUS FOR MONTH

1.
2.
3.

BRAIN DUMP

FOR THIS MONTH (THIS IS MY SAFE SPACE!)

THIS MONTH PRIORITES

FOR IMPACT THIS MONTH	FOR IMPACT NEXT MONTH
FOR IMPACT THIS QUARTER	FOR IMPACT LONGER TERM

MY QUARTERLY REFLECTION

Activity or goals I had to postpone during this quarter

THINGS that I need to try next quarter

MY
QUARTERLY
ACTIVITY

Q1	Q2	Q3	Q4

Content/ Keywords/ Hashtags

Q1	Q2	Q3	Q4

Content themes and ideas I'm focusing on

Keywords I need to use

Hashtag Bank

WEEKLY PLAN

Q1	Q2	Q3	Q4

Platform	Mon	Tues	Wed	Thurs	Fri	Sat	Sun
Email							

MY EMAIL PLAN

Q1	Q2	Q3	Q4

THE FOUR STEP PLAN

All emails need:
- ○ A short story
- ○ One call to action
- ○ Kept simple
- ○ Add value
- ○ Personalised it

WHAT IS MY SALE FOCUS?

Offer   %

1.

2.

3.

4.

My email focus	Tone/style	Offer/CTA
Week 1/5/9		
Week 2/6/10		
Week 3/7/11		
Week 4/8/12		

MY EMAIL PLAN

Q1	Q2	Q3	Q4

THE FOUR STEP PLAN

All emails need:
- ○ A short story
- ○ One call to action
- ○ Kept simple
- ○ Add value
- ○ Personalised it

WHAT IS MY SALE FOCUS?

Offer   %

1.

2.

3.

4.

My email focus	Tone/style	Offer/CTA
Week 1/5/9		
Week 2/6/10		
Week 3/7/11		
Week 4/8/12		

MY EMAIL PLAN

Q1	Q2	Q3	Q4

THE FOUR STEP PLAN

All emails need:
- ○ A short story
- ○ One call to action
- ○ Kept simple
- ○ Add value
- ○ Personalised it

WHAT IS MY SALE FOCUS?

Offer   %

1.

2.

3.

4.

My email focus	Tone/style	Offer/CTA
Week 1/5/9		
Week 2/6/10		
Week 3/7/11		
Week 4/8/12		

My core platform schedule

Platform	
Frequency	

Q1	Q2	Q3	Q4

Day of week	Time	Type	Format
Monday			
Tuesday			
Wednesday			
Thursday			
Friday			
Saturday			
Sunday			

Type:
Promo
FAQ
Social proof
How we work
About us
Relational Content
Reach/Noticed

Formats:
Carousel
Single Image in text
Meme
Video
Quotes
Testimonials
Reels/Short video
Animation

My MONTHLY ACTIVITY TRACKER

J F M A M J J A S O N D

Working ahead keeps us ON TRACK and IN CONTROL. Tick off as you work ahead.

Content type	Frequency	1	2	3	4	5	Date done
		☐	☐	☐	☐	☐	
		☐	☐	☐	☐	☐	
		☐	☐	☐	☐	☐	
		☐	☐	☐	☐	☐	
		☐	☐	☐	☐	☐	
		☐	☐	☐	☐	☐	
		☐	☐	☐	☐	☐	
		☐	☐	☐	☐	☐	
		☐	☐	☐	☐	☐	
		☐	☐	☐	☐	☐	
		☐	☐	☐	☐	☐	
		☐	☐	☐	☐	☐	
		☐	☐	☐	☐	☐	

My MONTHLY PLAN

J F M A M J J A S O N D

GRATITUDE FOCUS FOR MONTH

1.
2.
3.

B R A I N   D U M P

FOR THIS MONTH (THIS IS MY SAFE SPACE!)

THIS MONTH PRIORITES

FOR IMPACT THIS MONTH	FOR IMPACT NEXT MONTH
FOR IMPACT THIS QUARTER	FOR IMPACT LONGER TERM

My MONTHLY ACTIVITY TRACKER

J F M A M J J A S O N D

Working ahead keeps us ON TRACK and IN CONTROL. Tick off as you work ahead.

Content type	Frequency	1	2	3	4	5	Date done
		☐	☐	☐	☐	☐	
		☐	☐	☐	☐	☐	
		☐	☐	☐	☐	☐	
		☐	☐	☐	☐	☐	
		☐	☐	☐	☐	☐	
		☐	☐	☐	☐	☐	
		☐	☐	☐	☐	☐	
		☐	☐	☐	☐	☐	
		☐	☐	☐	☐	☐	
		☐	☐	☐	☐	☐	
		☐	☐	☐	☐	☐	
		☐	☐	☐	☐	☐	
		☐	☐	☐	☐	☐	
		☐	☐	☐	☐	☐	

My MONTHLY PLAN

J F M A M J J A S O N D

GRATITUDE FOCUS FOR MONTH

1.
2.
3.

B R A I N   D U M P

FOR THIS MONTH (THIS IS MY SAFE SPACE!)

THIS MONTH PRIORITES

FOR IMPACT THIS MONTH	FOR IMPACT NEXT MONTH
FOR IMPACT THIS QUARTER	FOR IMPACT LONGER TERM

My MONTHLY ACTIVITY TRACKER

J F M A M J J A S O N D

Working ahead keeps us ON TRACK and IN CONTROL. Tick off as you work ahead.

Content type	Frequency	1	2	3	4	5	Date done
		☐	☐	☐	☐	☐	
		☐	☐	☐	☐	☐	
		☐	☐	☐	☐	☐	
		☐	☐	☐	☐	☐	
		☐	☐	☐	☐	☐	
		☐	☐	☐	☐	☐	
		☐	☐	☐	☐	☐	
		☐	☐	☐	☐	☐	
		☐	☐	☐	☐	☐	
		☐	☐	☐	☐	☐	
		☐	☐	☐	☐	☐	
		☐	☐	☐	☐	☐	
		☐	☐	☐	☐	☐	

My MONTHLY PLAN

J F M A M J J A S O N D

GRATITUDE FOCUS FOR MONTH

1.

2.

3.

B R A I N   D U M P

FOR THIS MONTH (THIS IS MY SAFE SPACE!)

THIS MONTH PRIORITES

FOR IMPACT THIS MONTH	FOR IMPACT NEXT MONTH
FOR IMPACT THIS QUARTER	FOR IMPACT LONGER TERM

MY QUARTERLY REFLECTION

Activity or goals I had to postpone during this quarter

THINGS that I need to try next quarter

Looking ahead

Planning for Next Year

Take time looking through this planner before you jump into planning for the following twelve months,

Reflecting on what worked and what didn't
What lit you up, what dragged you down
Where you needed more support
What flowed and got results
What helped grow your business
What died a wee death

All of this will help you for next year.

It's worth the time.

BIG IDEAS FOR NEXT YEAR

Activity or goals I had to postpone until now

PIPE DREAMS, AMBITION, AND THINGS that I need to try

MISSES/OPPORTUNITIES I COULD DO BETTER	POPPED IN NEXT YEARS CALENDER

STUFF THAT BOMBED	ACTION/LEARNING

What I've grown in this year

my confidence

My mindset

My skill level

My wins

Progress *is* always progress

Sometimes our progress can feel so slow.
It's halted by things outside of our control.
It's held back by our distractions, our life, our busy-ness.

But small changes have great impact long term. If we want to build a sticky content web that makes getting new clients simple and easy, it's about building over time.

If you get discouraged about your progress, it's so good to look back and acknowledge:

You are not the same as you were 12 months ago
You've moved forward even in times you felt you were standing still
And now..
It's time to celebrate all the moments you took action even when you didn't feel like it, or when it was hard

And through it all - remember:
Kind Spiders get the best clients!

www.ingramcontent.com/pod-product-compliance
Lightning Source LLC
Chambersburg PA
CBHW050936210326

41597CB00036B/6194